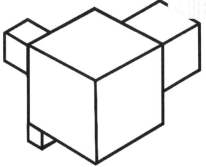

The Composable Roadmap

An action plan for agility in a modern digital marketplace

By Chad Solomonson and Greg Kihlström

Published by:

The Agile Brand

3100 Clarendon Boulevard #200

Arlington, VA 22201

https://www.agilebrandguide.com

First Edition: May 2024

The publisher is not responsible for websites (or their content) that are not owned by the publisher.

Cover Design and Illustrations by Greg Kihlström

Edited by Janelle Kihlström and Loretha Green

ISBN: 9-798-32498-166-2

Contents

Acknowledgements

Any work like this takes many to make it successful, and we are thankful to those we have worked with, specifically on this book, and those we have each worked with on related projects that have informed what was written in the pages that follow.

A big thank you to everyone who contributed to this book:

- **Chris Bach,** for the amazing foreword. Chris is the co-founder / CCO / CSO for Netlify. He started the company with his high school friend Matt Billman. Originally from Copenhagen, he noticed that the web experience would be more secure and scalable if it moved away from traditional monoliths to a new decoupled architecture. He is also the founder of the MACH Alliance.

- **Dominik Angerer,** for the insightful afterword. A web performance specialist and perfectionist. After working for big agencies as a full stack developer he founded Storyblok. He is also an active contributor to the open source community and one of the organizers of Scriptconf and Stahlstadt.js.

- **Lars Peterson** offered a grounded view of how development teams will need to integrate into composable architectures. He is the CEO and a co-founder of Uniform.dev. After acquiring in-depth expertise in personalizing and creating digital experiences at scale and content structure, he became interested in looking into ways to move composable architectures from early adoption to the mainstream. He is also co-author of "Connect – How to use data and experience marketing to create lifetime customers."

- **Jonathan Corley,** offers guidance from his experience advising industry-leading brands with a sharp focus on CX strategy and optimization. Jonathan is the Director of Experience Strategy, Customer Transformation at Sitecore. .

- **Michele Azar,** for sharing real-world retail examples on how composable actually gets internal momentum. Michele is an accomplished and visionary C-Suite executive who drives large-scale transformation and increased value for purpose-driven Fortune 500 brands such as Best Buy, WM, and MDI.

- **Leif Ulstrup** for insights on how Generative AI will connect into composable architectures. Leif is the founder of Primehook Technology. He served in executive roles at Computer Sciences Corporation (CSC), Deloitte Consulting, and American Management Systems (AMS). He is a member of the MIT Institute for Data, Systems, and Society (IDSS.mit.edu) advisory board.

- The RDA strategy team, with leadership from **Bill Buell and Lance Hayden**. This team continues to unlock speed and value for dozens of clients every year. The series of composable workshops that have been created serve as a clear path forward for both Marketing and IT leaders.

Huge hugs and love to our families. Without your support, this book doesn't happen.

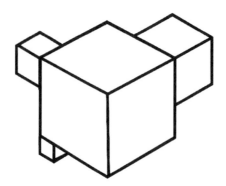

Foreword

"The future is composable."

"DXPs (digital experience platforms) are now built, not bought."

These quotes, from the largest tech analyst firms in the world, describe a fundamental shift in the preferred architecture for the web. It's happening at an incredible pace, making this the biggest shift since the collective move to the cloud (admittedly still ongoing, but unmistakably a mega trend in the last decade and a half).

So what is "composable architecture," what are best practices, where do you start, and why should you even care about it in the first place? To try to wrap around this, let's start by having a quick look at how it all came about.

In December 2013, my friend from high school and co-founder-to-be Matt Billmann reached out to me to hear my thoughts on an idea for a new architecture for the web.

The web was challenged back then. The architecture behind it was increasingly struggling to accommodate all the new needs and touchpoints constantly being developed. It scaled poorly, had ever-increasing security issues, and wasn't fast enough to cater to new platforms like smartphones.

The problem was that digital experiences back then were architected as so-called monoliths. The editing interface, business logic, website UI, templates, build tools, and more—all of it was made as one big piece of software that would sit on a server somewhere and build a contemporary version of a website, store, or app for every single visitor.

This resulted in a bottleneck with poor scalability, large security vulnerabilities as all the code running was exposed all the time, and enterprises were stuck on expensive solutions. If they wanted to change one aspect, like how content was managed, they would have to lift and shift to another monolith in its entirety, something that could often take years and be very expensive.

Omni-channel was becoming increasingly important, and the more digital touch points being added, the more bloated monolithic platforms became in their attempts to cater to the many different use cases, which ended up introducing a lot of compromises and being best in class at nothing. This also led to increased time to market, much to the frustration of marketers and digital product owners across the globe.

All these challenges were, in turn, leading to walled gardens such as mobile app stores and social media company pages as the web increasingly struggled. I felt the issues firsthand as I'd been working in digital agencies for more than a decade and was eager to find out if an architectural shift could resolve this.

The idea was, in essence, to decouple the frontend from the backend, essentially to split the site or presentation layer or UI away from the backend, data, and business logic. This has already been proven in principle to be a successful approach for smartphones.

When Steve Jobs first presented the iPhone (as a PDF), all the screen icons were shortcuts to websites. The notion of an app didn't exist. However, we collectively found out that pulling in the

UI every time you turned a page was never going to scale. The phones and mobile broadband weren't fast enough for the existing web architecture to work. Instead, we ended up pre-building an app, running it on the phone's operating system, and then connecting to APIs and microservices for anything that needed real-time updating, like comments or putting in payment info.

It turned out that if we could bring this decoupling to the web as well, it could have a tremendous impact for a handful of reasons:

Instead of a monolith running everything from a single server, you could build more upfront and have multiple points of origin.

- This would give you better scalability, faster load times, and better security.

Your web developers would get superpowers.

- Instead of having to hand over a frontend for implementation into a backend (often waiting months to get back experiences that looked only a little like the original layout due to template restraints, etc.), you would simply pull the data from the backend into the frontend.

- This cut down time to market significantly, gave a lot higher fidelity in designs, and cut down on resources needed to go live.

Lastly, it would pave the way towards composable solutions.

- This means that enterprises could have the flexibility to build highly customized stacks, where interchangeability would be king.
- No more lifting and shifting of an entire marketing stack just because they needed functionality that their current solution didn't offer. Instead, they would just replace/add the needed component.
- This agility would be key to having a faster time to market, reducing overhead, and better supporting omnichannel.

Of course, for all this to happen, an entire ecosystem would have to be built out. Simply put, there could, for example, be no composable commerce if all commerce solutions remained built out as monoliths.

In addition, there would need to be a rethink of how all these components were connected and operated. Without an orchestration platform, there wouldn't really be viable and scalable use cases.

We set out to build the latter at Netlify, premiering the first frontend cloud on the market.

Back then, we were a handful of companies in the new nascent category, but fast forward to today, and everything has changed.

There hasn't been a Content Management System or e-commerce solution provider in the last 4 years that isn't natively headless and composable.

The Gartners and Foresters of the world are predicting composable as a default architecture within a few years and deem enterprises that stay behind on monoliths as being at a significant competitive disadvantage.

At Netlify, we've seen the category get traction firsthand as well and now serve almost 5 million businesses and developers running more than 35 million sites, stores, and apps.

This all happened because the ecosystem went from a handful of vendors to thousands of service providers. Today, you can build anything and everything in a composable manner. Your marketing and commerce services are all available in headless and composable forms, both from existing vendors that used to offer the same services as monoliths and, of course, as new players on the scene.

Now, AI is rapidly disrupting the digital scene again. Composable architecture is needed to embrace the new AI tooling and services that are arriving rapidly, bringing game-changing opportunities with them. Without it, you don't have the flexibility to integrate these new technologies and services as they come along.

As with any new category, standards are still being written out, and best practices are still being established. While going composable is a must for any marketer or digital product owner who wants agility and adaptability in their digital solutions, finding out where to start and how to create the right business cases can be overwhelming.

In addition, few enterprises have the luxury of only doing greenfield projects. Most have a ton of existing digital services that they either can't or don't want to get rid of, so understanding how to build composable in a way that co-exists and integrates with existing solutions is often of the essence as well.

Those are the reasons for this book. It's a concrete guide that takes the reader through the what and how in tangible ways for digital product owners, marketers, and architects alike.

The future isn't written, but it is indeed composable.

Chris Bachman

Co-founder & CSO at Netlify

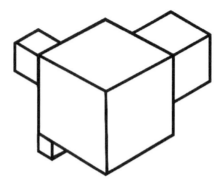

It is not the strongest of the species that survives,

nor the most intelligent that survives. It is the one

that is the most adaptable to change.

—Charles Darwin

Introduction:
The composable journey

Last year, Amazon knocked out yet another historic retail brand, Bed Bath and Beyond. They were too slow to invest in omnichannel strategies and missed the opportunity to capitalize on the convenience of e-commerce shopping. Overstock then paid $21.5 million to acquire Bed Bath & Beyond's intellectual property and applied that value to its agile platform. Overstock.com CEO Jonathan Johnson said, "The combination of our winning asset-light business model and the high awareness and loyalty of the Bed Bath & Beyond brand will improve the customer experience and position the company for accelerated market share growth."

Five years before the transaction, Overstock had already been building a roadmap that enabled real-time personalization between channels to ensure their customers would have a fast and easy digital experience. Overstock was wired for change and, like Amazon, sought areas to increase speed and market share.

Around the same time Overstock was making moves, Gartner made this bold forecast: **"The future of business is composable."** They advised businesses to follow composable principles such as creating "swappable building blocks" to adjust to global events, market disruptions, and changes quickly and easily in consumer preferences.

This book surfaces how businesses are embracing composable thinking, building tech stacks that are more agile and organizing teams that work towards common digital goals. These are the core pillars of creating and leveraging a composable roadmap ready for growth, change, and speed!

Who is this book for?

When we first started to structure this book, we noticed that marketing and IT leaders were hiring both external consultants and internal marketing operations employees to bridge these two important departments. This book is for those marketing technology "bridge builders." You can see this role playing out in Marketing Operations roles. These brave leaders want to align with business goals, build marketing strategies that embrace speed to market, and understand how systems and data need to connect. They are ultimately passionate about the customer experience and helping their companies grow.

> ### *What do you need to be a successful bridge builder?*
>
> - A clear vision of success (answer the WHY)
> - The courage to manage and lead change
> - Ability to drive consensus across different departments
> - The confidence to understand technology
> - A team of internal and external experts

We have both delivered dozens of digital roadmaps over the last decade but see an emerging and critical need to drive technology acumen into roadmaps. We wrote this book to ignite new conversations and ideas into modern marketing strategies. We offer some composable best practices and guidance on composable-focused workshops to support getting started. Ultimately, the goal is to continue to support the path to delighting customers and growing successful businesses.

What problems are we solving?

We know that marketing technologies that rely on outdated and rigid software platforms make it painful for businesses to keep up with the pace and flexibility needed to thrive in today's competitive market.

New features are hard and costly, or even impossible, to add. Integrating with other back-office systems to enhance the order processing experience takes too much time and resources, leaving systems disconnected and underutilized. And when a new go-to-market strategy or opportunity emerges, teams must start from scratch and select vendors again. To avoid these challenges, you need to rethink your strategy before your competitors do. You need technology designed with flexibility and scalability so that you can modify, access new markets, and maintain control of the customer experience over time. You need the ability to own your roadmap.

The marketing operations role was mainly developed to deal with technology already put in place without a lot of strategy around its original implementation. Because that software was being siloed, marketing operations teams frequently asked questions such as:

- How can we improve the customer experience?
- How do we demonstrate more value from these application channels?
- Where can we consolidate investments?
- How secure is the data that is moving across all these applications?
- What technology partners 'fit' our goals and plans?

And what about you? Think about your current digital

strategy. Maybe you have technical debt (the real cost of rework caused by choosing the quickest solution rather than the most effective solution) and are pressured to provide modern technology to deliver better customer experiences. Maybe you're concerned about being locked in with your vendor, who currently dictates how you can innovate. Maybe you are thinking about trying to consolidate the hodgepodge of solutions in your environment. Or maybe you're simply spending too much time and money and not getting anywhere close to the desired results.

There is good news. Technology vendors and cloud software providers are finally architecting their solutions to become easier to integrate and consolidate, allowing for more mitigation of the risks associated with vendor lock-in, multiple cloud platforms, and data security. Ultimately, these changes have created opportunities for businesses to build partnerships specific to their unique customer needs. For so long, marketers and IT have been reactive...now they have access to creating a plan that is developed to think through how to solve these challenges more agile and... is proactive.

What exactly is a composable roadmap?

Most digital roadmaps today are not fixed since many things can change quickly with technology, the competitive environment, and the organization itself. A composable roadmap can be seen as a vital step between the approval of a digital strategy and the execution of investments and work that delivers on that strategy. It is important to remember that composability is a journey, not a destination. Every leading company in their respective industries continues to invest in better customer experience, experimentation, speed to market, and agility.

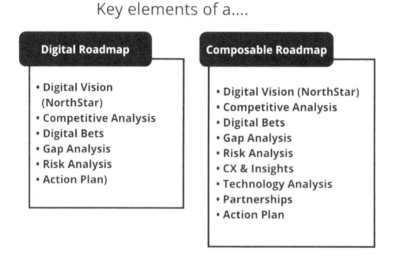

Figure 0.1, Key elements of a digital roadmap and composable roadmap

We have engaged with several technology experts while writing this book. Each chapter provides best practices and insights from these business and technology leaders to support your efforts.

We hope the pages ahead will provide some shape to what a modern roadmap could look like for composability in your business. The following chapters will support your ability to develop a foundational strategy, better understand important building blocks to consider, and provide guidance on measuring outcomes along the way.

More insights for the journey

From Michele Azar, Digital Transformation Executive, on building the composable business case

There are three main drivers of the business case for a composable approach – Speed to market, customer satisfaction, and cost savings. A great way to view the business case is to consider the benefits for rapid prototyping – fail fast, pilot quickly, invent with new tools.

The composable approach adds more toys to the toybox. Think about the pieces as Lego blocks or toys created by combinations of components or brand differentiators – You can easily click in a piece and if it doesn't work, you take it out and snap in another component and see if that solves the issue.

You can iterate super-fast with no code by just connecting systems with one another and disconnect and connect very quickly but with traditional code you cannot.

Another digitally powered enabler is the ability to say, yes, we have that product, when would you like it? As part of a composable roadmap, access to inventory and inventory availability is also critical. In early 2000 Best Buy piloted and launched Buy Online Pickup Instore but didn't finish the inventory capability until 2012 when 20% of the time customers were getting an out-of-stock message online when in fact Best Buy had the inventory in store. The sourcing logic and ability to keep the customer order delivery date promise sourced based on the get-it-by date and zip code proved game-changing both in 2012 and in 2020 when the pandemic hit. The impact of this flexible, composable inventory capability drove impact in the billions of revenue and corresponding margin improvement – enabling the use of digital sourcing to sell products sooner.

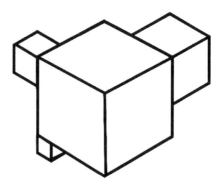

"A good way to think about composability is the creation of building blocks and frameworks when combined drive differentiation."

—Michele Azar

Part 1
Foundational strategy:
What you need to know

Let's start our exploration of what you need to know about a composable strategy and the inputs you will need to build your roadmap.

What are the elements of a good roadmap?

Most digital roadmaps move through three key phases—visioning a high-level strategy and business justification, activating the initiatives and minimum-viable products, and scaling across the organization.

5 essential deliverables of a digital roadmap

- Digital Vision (North Star)
- Competitive Positioning
- Prioritized Initiatives
- Gap & Risk Analysis
- Roadmap

Figure 1.0, Five essential deliverables of a digital roadmap

A solid digital roadmap typically connects five essential deliverables, as shown in figure 1.0. Let's explore each in a little more depth:

1. **Digital Vision (North Star)**. How is digital changing your industry? What new offerings, operating models, and business models can it enable? What is possible?
2. **Competitive Positioning.** How is digital affecting competitive advantage? Where are we well positioned? Where are we disadvantaged? What do customers love about you?
3. **Prioritized List Top Initiatives**. Which digital opportunities are consistent with your business strategy based on speed to value potential? In what order should you pursue them?
4. **Gap & Risk Analysis.** What gaps in capabilities, organization, and systems need to be filled to be successful?
5. **Roadmap.** What are the timelines, targets, and accountabilities for each of your programs? What moves are needed to fund the journey?

These outputs form a coherent and compatible framework of decisions that integrate digital strategy with business strategy—and link implementation closely to both.

"The business case for a composable approach lies in its ability to optimize speed to market for brands, facilitating faster launches of digital experiences when executed correctly. Unlike tightly coupled workflows where tasks are interdependent, a composable approach optimizes delivery workflows by allowing for decoupled streams in design, code, content, and experience management.

Lars Peterson, CEO of Uniform

What are the goals for adding composable capabilities?

The variety of software options has resulted in a surge of customized architectures, where customers select the components that best suit their business needs. Why? Standardized, all-in-one software platforms won't create an edge over competitors. Standardization leads to uniformity.

Customer expectations continue to change rapidly. In the age of just about anything being available through next-day delivery, customers don't like to wait too long for things. Because they enjoy nearly endless customization of everything from cars to fashion, they expect things to be personalized to their liking. They want content, offers, and experiences when, where, and how they want them. If you want to be successful, you'll need to implement an efficient way of identifying and exceeding those expectations.

The business value of a composable approach to marketing technology infrastructure cannot be ignored. It brings a whole host of value points that ideally deliver more revenue and more margins to the business. Goals for building composability into the roadmap include:

Speed and Efficiency

One of the primary benefits of a composable approach to marketing technology infrastructure is speed and efficiency. This allows organizations to experiment with new technologies and marketing channels, enabling them to gain insights into what works best. Additionally, a composable approach requires less time and resources to build new solutions and integrate them with existing systems, which ultimately allows companies to execute campaigns faster than their competitors.

Flexibility

By adopting a modular approach, businesses can quickly swap out components as needed without having to rebuild entire systems. This ensures that organizations can respond to changing market dynamics or customer behavior promptly and efficiently. For example, if a particular marketing channel is no longer effective, a composable approach enables companies to pivot and allocate resources elsewhere quickly.

Consistency

Consistency is crucial in ensuring customers have an excellent brand experience across different channels. By using common APIs, data formats, and user interfaces, businesses can ensure that all touchpoints with their customers are consistent and aligned with their brand messaging. This results in a highly effective and unified brand experience across multiple channels, ultimately driving customer loyalty and increasing sales.

Do we have the right leadership to deliver this approach?

Regardless of your organizational structure, success with

composability starts at the top. This can be your greatest advantage or challenge. You need to have executive buy-in on this type of approach. Speaking with executives, when you're talking about speed to market, potential cost savings as it relates to the consultant, and internal overhead cost through the potential streamlining of applications, as well as potential benefit to the customer, you typically have a win-win-win.

There are several stakeholders that you will need to support your composable roadmap, as pictured in Figure 1.1. First, however, you want to have executive buy-in. We are seeing increased involvement by the CFO or COO earlier in the process because there are so many potential cost savings benefits.

Key stakeholders

· Chief Executive Officer
· Marketing Leadership
· IT Leadership
· Marketing Ops
· E-commerce Leadership
· Procurement
· New Partnerships

Figure 1.1, Key stakeholders in the composable roadmap

What roles & skillsets are required?

We recommend having a champion, someone who is a product owner around composability, someone who is aligned with the company's North Star vision.

Different factors, such as the company's specific requirements, the sector it belongs to, and the scope of the effort, may affect the makeup of a typical 'dream team.' However, some essential roles are usually part of a transformation project team:

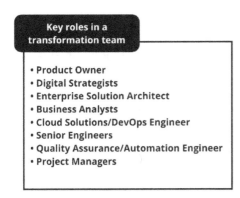

Key roles in a transformation team

- Product Owner
- Digital Strategists
- Enterprise Solution Architect
- Business Analysts
- Cloud Solutions/DevOps Engineer
- Senior Engineers
- Quality Assurance/Automation Engineer
- Project Managers

Figure 1.2, Key roles in a transformation team

It is also recommended to look at external implementation partners who have deep technology experience and are comfortable with cloud development and scalable architectures. Many companies are challenged to bring on full-time employees, so they look for longer-term, strategic relationships with partners. ensuring that what the partner is delivering is truly what's needed at the time.

As a company looks to bolt on additional capabilities, it may make more sense to bring those resources inside. But more than likely, you'll be looking at more analysts and more strategists because you're able to have such confidence in moving in and out of technology that, really, it's a matter of the outcomes and the partners will help to find those outcomes about what the company needs. And so that's a strong vision of how the resourcing can play out.

Another thing to consider is that, as you're looking at new ways of procuring different types of solutions, you're going to want to have some legal support from your team to ensure that you are starting to build contractual arrangements that are easier to onboard and offboard so that, as you become more confident in your environment.

How do I build a bridge between marketing & IT?

The relationship between Marketing and IT leaders can be difficult, but it is critical to success. What we know is that business leaders only care about the outcomes of marketing technology, such as revenue growth from omnichannel experiences and personalized experiences that create loyalty while also lowering the costs to acquire customers.

These initiatives all require the ability to get data insights. However, the data is typically managed by IT. IT collects, organizes, secures, and cleans the data to make it available for different business functions. From that perspective, IT's cooperation with marketing is very important to provide the right data and choose the underlying platforms and technology on which all these initiatives depend. Teamwork is certainly needed.

We have found that establishing common 'tenets for success' between Marketing and IT is a great way to build accountability and trust together.

Some examples of tenets include:

- 'We will always seek to create happy and loyal customers.'
- 'We will always align our digital goals to business goals.'
- 'We will always secure data in a responsible way.'
- 'We will strive to leverage technologies with proven

APIs.'

Documenting tenets will establish expectations upfront. Also, agreeing on a common language will ensure that both teams build a composable mindset (see next chapter. MACH Mindset).

Roadmap checklist: Foundational strategy

Here are some important roadmap reminders when crafting your foundational strategy:

People (e.g., customers, key stakeholders, teammates, partners, and communities)

☐ What are the skills and experience gaps? Do we need to make strategic hires to guide our technology talent and help the managers within the functions of the business to prepare them to participate in building modules?

☐ Do we have the right technology provider relationships that share our vision and will work as partners, not just vendors?

☐ Conduct interviews with internal business

stakeholders to discuss current pain points, vision for the future, and digital goals.

Process (e.g., change management, agile/scrum, cadences, communications, KPIs)

☐ Start to conduct interviews with business stakeholders to discuss current pain points, vision for the future, and platform goals.

Technology (e.g., Software Platforms, AI, Dashboards, etc.)

☐ Perform an audit of your current martech applications.

☐ Identify areas where increased adaptability, connected data, or business user interfaces could yield efficiency gains or drive new revenue.

Risk Mitigation (e.g., internal and external forces)

☐ Perform an audit of your current martech applications.

☐ Identify areas where increased adaptability, connected data, or business user interfaces could yield efficiency gains or drive new revenue.

More insights for the journey

From Lars Pederson, CEO and a cofounder of Uniform.dev, on building the composable business case.

The business case for a composable approach lies in its ability to optimize speed to market for brands, facilitating faster launches of digital experiences when executed correctly. Unlike tightly coupled workflows where tasks are interdependent, a composable approach optimizes delivery workflows by allowing for decoupled streams in design, code, content, and experience management. These streams operate independently but seamlessly connect when the experience is launched. This flexibility transforms the pace at which projects can be delivered, granting brands the freedom to prioritize aspects like design systems, content, or experience based on their specific needs.

When establishing a composable approach, it's crucial to recognize that it doesn't spontaneously occur simply by having multiple systems with fast APIs labeled as "composable." The success of composable technologies hinges on having a corresponding composable architecture. This necessitates a platform that facilitates the connection, orchestration, and delivery of digital experiences in a composable manner. Without such a platform, brands may find themselves with a solution assembled through custom coding, essentially forming a custom monolith where any modifications can become costly.

While substantial business benefits are associated with a composable approach, it's essential to acknowledge that it may not be suitable for everyone. Executing composability correctly requires mature enterprise architects who comprehend the needs of both developers and marketers. These architects should be focused on constructing a scalable platform that not only enables composability in the present but also in the future.

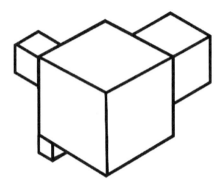

A composable roadmap defines your path and technology rather than letting the technology define you.

Part 2
The building blocks

Building an agile ecosystem of technologies that specifically aligns with your unique business requirements builds more confidence in how you are going to procure the types of solutions that you need and that fit your growth projections.

Just like a software company builds a roadmap for how they think about building value from their software, any company with a composable approach needs to think that way and create a roadmap that considers their variety of needs.

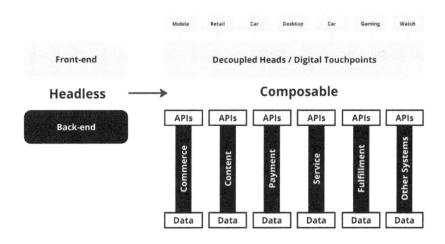

Figure 2.1, How headless and composable relate to one another

With your composable roadmap strategy in place, you will need to evaluate the platforms that will make up your infrastructure. The upside? More flexibility and choice in platforms that can give you best-in-class functionality. The downside? There are more platforms to evaluate and some tough decisions to make! Let's explore this a bit more.

What are 'systems of connectedness' ?

Over a decade ago, Gartner introduced the Pace-Layered Application Strategy, a methodology for categorizing, managing, and governing applications to foster business change, differentiation, and innovation. This strategy helped organizations develop tailored strategies by distinguishing between systems of record, differentiation, and innovation.

As digital partnerships evolved with the advancement of cloud frameworks and APIs, these connections have become more integral, leading to the concept of 'Systems of Connectedness'. The 'API-first' approach treats APIs as standalone products that foster innovation by enabling easy access to data and functionality, which speeds up development without the need to build features from scratch.

There are many benefits to using an API-first approach.

APIs speed up the development process by providing easy access to data and functionality. Development teams use the APIs to take advantage of the value the APIs offer and avoid having to create the functionality themselves.

The systems that have already built solid APIs are winning and staying highly 'connected' into enterprise stacks.

Do you have a 'MACH' mindset?

> *"Future-proof enterprise technology and drive new digital experiences."* - MACH Alliance Manifesto

A MACH mindset is about how you incorporate the unique value of your company so that you can move faster and give a better experience to your customers, so that you don't get stuck into long implementation, upgrade, or migrations projects.

MACH is about integration and how services and data are moving back and forth. For those less familiar with the term, let's just briefly define what MACH stands for (*also see the glossary for more definitions)*:

Microservices

Microservices refer to a software development approach where software systems are broken down into smaller independent modules that can operate separately and communicate with each other through APIs.

As it relates to marketers, this means that every component of an application can be moved or scaled up and down to meet the changing needs of the business. This enables marketers to create targeted campaigns that can be rapidly deployed and adapted to changing customer needs.

API-first

As discussed earlier, this approach enables developers to focus on building a flexible, scalable API that can serve a wide range of functions. Marketers can then leverage this API to access and use data in different ways to create personalized user experiences, such as targeted ads, product recommendations, and more. API-first architecture enables marketers to test, iterate, and roll out new features and campaigns faster.

Cloud-Native SaaS

Cloud-native SaaS refers to a cloud-based approach to software development and deployment. This means that applications are created and run in the cloud environment, allowing for fast and flexible deployment, scaling, and management.

Marketers can benefit from cloud-native SaaS architecture by being able to access their applications from anywhere and at any time. Moreover, cloud-native SaaS enables marketers to easily integrate third-party tools and services, which can be crucial in today's omnichannel marketing world.

Headless

Headless refers to separating the frontend of an application (such as the user interface) from its backend (such as the software and data). In simpler terms, headless architecture enables developers and marketers to create and manage content independently of the platform that delivers it.

This means that marketers can personalize content without the need for complex web development skills. With headless architecture, marketers can focus on crafting the perfect message for their audience rather than having to navigate technical complexities.

To learn more about having a MACH mindset, check out the MACH Alliance. They are a not-for-profit industry body that advocates for open and best-of-breed enterprise technology ecosystems.

What type of partners should we work with?

In today's environment, partnering should be highly collaborative, with a focus on transparency and alignment of business objectives. Choose partners who understand your business and can contribute to your digital transformation strategy effectively. It's crucial that these partners not only share your vision but also have relevant experience and expertise to help you navigate and scale your digital transformation efforts successfully.

Taking a composable approach means that marketing and IT teams are no longer stuck with legacy features and outdated monolithic systems, and because of this, companies want to consolidate only what they're truly using. As they look to partner with integrators and agencies and consultancies, they must align their thinking in the same way with these partners, and many of these partners may also be developing new business models that support more ongoing value, that add to investments and that are aligned with a partner company's objectives and way of thinking. These outside partners will be very supportive of a roadmap and may even have considerable experience building a similar one. .

The goal is to create a pool of experienced, qualified resources aligned with your specific goals, objectives, and timelines to deploy and scale digital transformation. This benefit becomes increasingly important as you move along the digital transformation journey and the challenges become more complex.

An important component of partnerships is finding partners and solution providers with similar use cases and vertical expertise. It is becoming increasingly important now that these partners can speak your language and understand the real use cases you are trying to solve. This drives additional value, understanding, and support. You want to be able to ensure that they understand your business so that they can determine where composability can start and then continue to scale from there.

What are some typical delivery approaches?

Utilizing agile principles, realized in many forms, has become the best practice for software delivery in the market now. This still applies here. Most companies understand agile, even if they have not formally adopted big-A "Agile" principles and methods based on them. The mentality of agile for delivering on sprints and having the right resourcing available during those sprints is a solid and proven approach. This continues to be true when moving to a composable approach.

Sprints can be executed in various ways, and effective

upfront planning, particularly around MACH principles, is crucial. This ensures that architectural guidelines and standards are established, enabling scrum teams to operate more efficiently. Moreover, such planning enhances the value and speed of sprints, leading to quicker releases than currently achieved.

The beauty of composable is that the migration process isn't one-size-fits-all. Businesses can move at their own pace and decide which components to change, plus when and how to go about these changes. This is where assessments and workshop findings become crucial for growth. *See Part 3 for Workshop Ideas.*

Where does Gen AI fit into the roadmap?

"The emergence of Gen AI and the ease with which technology novices can create and test sophisticated working software modules will make those options more abundant. Those with business acumen and expertise and the ability to craft Gen AI prompts that shape the development of a component of a composable platform will shift to the driver's seat in how enterprise applications are configured and operate." —Lief Ulstrup, Primehook Technology

To use Gen AI effectively, organizations need to integrate the different technologies that are involved in handling product data smoothly. Proper product information needs a flexible, modular system where different software services can be chosen, combined, and modified as needed. AI algorithms depend on data.

As Gen AI applications often need to access multiple systems and data sources, a composable commerce framework allows retailers to create a central repository for all product data by connecting their PIM, ERP, OMS, DAM, and other systems easily, making product data readily available to these AI applications.

This integrated data environment allows retailers to create a base of rich product information, including descriptions, attributes, images, and pricing, to enable AI algorithms to use correct, complete, and current information to generate dynamic pricing, personalized recommendations, targeted marketing campaigns, and other smart functionalities. With a composable framework, organizations can manage and activate their whole product record across all channels without being slowed down by the complexity of their tech stack, the number of custom integrations they have created, or the number of stakeholders involved.

Composable technology and generative AI are creating amazing opportunities for innovation and creativity when used together. Think about how you could use Gen AI to make customized products, services, or experiences that suit your audience. The modular, composable principles of AI and composable architectures are redefining business operations, creating a powerful landscape.

These architectures, characterized by their modular nature, allow organizations to select and assemble various components or services like building blocks, creating a tailored system that precisely fits their unique requirements. The integration of Generative AI into this composable framework opens a new realm of possibilities, enhancing personalization, content creation, and decision-making processes, thereby revolutionizing how companies interact with their customers and optimize their operations.

Generative AI, with its ability to create content, predict trends, and personalize customer experiences, becomes a powerhouse when plugged into a composable architecture. It acts as a dynamic component that can be continuously evolved and adapted without overhauling the entire system. For instance, an e-commerce platform can leverage generative AI to produce product descriptions, recommend products, or even generate personalized marketing copy, responding in real-time to the shifting sands of market trends and consumer preferences. This capability not only increases efficiency and effectiveness but also enables a level of personalization and responsiveness that was previously unattainable, leading to enhanced customer engagement and satisfaction.

The composable nature of these architectures means that generative AI can be seamlessly integrated with other components, such as CRM systems, analytics tools, and customer service bots, creating a cohesive and intelligent ecosystem. This integration facilitates a holistic approach to data analysis and utilization, where insights gained from one component can inform the actions of others. For example, data from customer interactions can be used to train the GenAI, improving its accuracy and relevance in real-time, which in turn can drive more personalized marketing strategies, optimized product offerings, and improved customer experiences.

The combination of GenAI and composable architectures signals a new phase for marketing technology and e-commerce. It gives businesses the flexibility to innovate and respond to market changes, the ability to offer unparalleled levels of customization, and the resources to create more productive, impactful, and appealing customer experiences. As organizations plan for the future, the incorporation of these technologies will not just be a competitive edge but a basic necessity to remain pertinent and thrive in the fast-changing digital landscape.

How to measure ongoing success

To evaluate the effectiveness of a composable approach, look at the following key indicators:

- **Time and cost:** An effectively implemented composable system should demonstrate a reduction in both time and cost compared to conventional methods. This efficiency is due to the modular nature of composable systems, which allows for rapid assembly and integration of different components. By streamlining these processes, organizations can achieve quicker deployment and lower initial costs, providing a clear, measurable advantage over traditional, monolithic systems. This initial assessment not only sets the baseline for operational efficiency but also highlights the cost-effectiveness of adopting a composable approach in the early stages of implementation.

- **Employee satisfaction:** Measuring team satisfaction is a crucial indicator of the effectiveness of composable development. It provides insights into the experiences and sentiments of developers and marketers, particularly in terms of their ability to efficiently create and launch projects. Positive feedback in this area not only signifies a successful composable implementation but also often correlates with improved productivity and creativity among team members. Enhanced satisfaction from smoother project executions can lead to better job fulfillment and lower turnover rates, further indicating the strategic benefits of adopting a composable framework.

- **Architecture flexibility:** Evaluate the architecture's true composability by measuring the ease and speed of swapping one content source for another. In an effectively composable architecture, this swap should be straightforward and leave frontend components unchanged. Conversely, reliance on custom coding and direct connections between frontend components and specific content sources may suggest reduced flexibility and effectiveness.

When considering composability, we're enhancing efficiency in handling similar products. For example, in e-commerce, while the success metrics remain the same, composability allows for more efficient operations and enhanced customer engagement compared to legacy solutions.

There is going to have to be a shift in how companies procure, as well as the speed of unlocking the value. For instance, you can go in and turn on a content stack and have a site up in five minutes. That's real today. But you couldn't do that with some of the major digital experience platform (DXP) players today. That's the shift with composable. That's the speed.

It's no longer nine-to-twelve-month deployments; it's two, three months. Speed of deployment is the bigger factor here, but the value points are the same. If it's a commerce solution, you're looking for growth in commerce; you're looking for revenue. If it's a loyalty application or a search, you're looking for more engagement. You're looking for cross-sell, upsell goals, and those all change, right? But they're going to be the same across those solutions.

Now, let's look at how we can measure success with a composable approach. Measuring speed can be difficult. With most KPIs, you can point back to conversions or transactional revenue, but there are some softer KPIs around engagement, loyalty subscriptions, registrations, and similar metrics. You'll likely see more and more measurements in things such as the speed of onboarding and offboarding new solutions, how quickly release cycles occur within the company, and whether they are a matter of days or even minutes.

The speed of that is where that agility starts to really unlock more revenue, more margin within a company. Ultimately, that's what everyone's looking at, so tying it back to those two, wherever possible, makes the most sense around success metrics. But speed is a big area where you'll see much more innovation and commitment.

What internal questions should I ask?

It's important to have confidence in what the current "As-Is" technology environment looks like. An audit of the technology, processes, and people will help frame your initial ideas and planning.

There are several questions that should be considered. Here is a good list to start with:

- On average, how long does it take your team to conceive, design, develop, and launch a website or digital product?
- In the past five years, has your team implemented any headless technology, i.e., an architecture in which content from one system is distributed to one or more

endpoints for presentation?

- Can your organization's line of business or functional leaders—e.g., your CMO—make updates to frontend experiences with their own frontend developers without having to rely on IT resources?

- Are the frontend components for your public-facing website available for reuse by other business functions, e.g., sales enablement, support, product management, and employee engagement?

- Or are multiple internal teams creating functionally similar experiences using unique, redundant components?

- Does your organization have teams or departments that work exclusively with a particular vendor? Are you beholden to those teams when work needs to be performed on those platforms?

- Does your vendor and software procurement policy prefer shorter licensing and subscription terms—e.g., 12 or 24 months—to maintain the flexibility to swap out technology in a relatively short timeframe when better or less expensive technology becomes available?

- Does your organization employ a "separation of concerns" approach in which application modules—e.g., user authentication—are loosely coupled to minimize the impact on other modules, enabling easier integration into other projects?

- Does your current staff have composability skills and experience with microservices, Jamstack, serverless, API, composable, decoupled, headless, etc.?
- Does your organization employ cross-functional governance and operate in ways that lead to collaboration and component reuse?

Roadmap checklist: The building blocks

People

- [ ] Assess your organizational readiness. Ensure that your team possesses the requisite skills and expertise needed.
- [ ] Define and document the types of partnerships that align with your business goals, culture, and industry.
- [ ] Build closer relationships with internal procurement teams and finance teams.

Process

- [ ] Define standards and governance regarding data and security.
- [ ] Build specific procurement policies that enable you

to be more agile with partners.

Technology

- [ ] Perform an audit on your applications and get confident on the current environment.
- [ ] Establish new components that need to be added to deliver the required business capabilities.
- [ ] Identify the components of your existing system that can be modularized or decoupled. These may include APIs, microservices, databases, and frontend applications.
- [ ] Determine the financial benefits of being in a particular cloud versus another.
- [ ] Evaluate where GenAI fits into current tech investments (*See Part 3 on GenAI workshop ideas*)

Risk Mitigation

- [ ] Define standards and governance regarding customer data and security.
- [ ] Build specific procurement policies that enable you to be more agile with partners.

CHAD SOLOMONSON & GREG KIHLSTRÖM | 64

More Gen AI insights for the journey

From Lief Ulstrap, Founder of Primehook Technology

Treat this journey as a series of experiments where you can learn and progress toward this vision and control the variables and risks as you proceed. It may be slower at the start, and the benefits narrower than a "big bang" approach to adoption, but you will increase your chances of success while you learn. The technology enabling this shift is also changing rapidly. The rise of GenAI adds a new wrinkle that will likely have significant ripple effects on IT architectures and the economics of software development, testing, and maintenance.

The most significant factors to move towards a composability are the economic incentives, widespread adoption of standard approaches to APIs, and the abundance of easy-to-program technologies to create specialized modules and cloud hosting options. The desire to achieve a "Lego blocks" approach to enterprise-grade software applications has been a dream for decades that was hard to realize in practice.

The emergence of generative AI (GenAI) and the ease with which technology novices can create and test sophisticated working software modules will make those options more abundant. Those with business acumen and expertise and the ability to craft GenAI prompts that shape the development of a component of a composable platform will shift to the driver's seat in how enterprise applications are configured and operate.

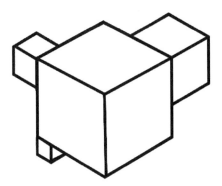

"As you consider composable solutions, take inventory of costs, capturing both one-time and recurring expenses in order to gain a clear view of TCO and projected benefits."

—Jonathan Corely, Director of Experience Strategy, Customer Transformation at Sitecore

Part 3
Getting started with workshops that work

With an understanding of the building blocks in place and an evaluation of both the current state as well as the desired end state, it is time to begin building your composable roadmap.

For the past 10 years, we have found that defined, bite-sized workshops are a great way to start building the key elements of the composable roadmap. Unlike regular meetings, workshops involve active participation and focused efforts to accomplish specific tasks or challenges. **Workshops can serve as powerful catalysts for creating successful digital products and solving complex challenges.**

Workshops are powerful opportunities for teams to unify and build consensus. These workshops facilitate cross-functional collaboration and knowledge sharing by bringing together key stakeholders from different departments, teams, or companies. Participants can learn from each other's experiences, exchange ideas, and build valuable connections to benefit the organization in the long run.

Workshops can be done in person or remotely. The power of in-person workshops is still unmatched, as they create an energy exchange that virtual sessions lack. However, remote workshops can also be effective with the right approach, for example, by introducing peak moments.

Workshop facilitators should be skilled at engaging participants, managing time effectively, and adapting to different personalities.

Let's explore four workshops that we recommend engaging in with the teams involved. We'll look at each and explore:

- An overview of the workshop
- The goals of the workshop
- The ideal participants in the workshop
- The recommended format
- The ideal outcomes of the workshop

Workshop 1: The art of the possible

In today's environment, many enterprise teams need a real jolt of inspiration and emotion. A clear vision of how customers can engage with them. They need to explore questions like "Imagine if...?" or "What if...?"

The Art of the Possible Workshop aims to get stakeholders unified and excited about customer growth, what they can do with modern technology, and how to unlock value from data and analytics. It helps them spot opportunities across their organization, and most importantly, it gets them to prioritize a list of potential workstreams so they can get 'unstuck' and move forward.

The goal of this workshop is threefold:

1. Get stakeholders aligned with a vision and possible impact modern technology can have.
2. Gather a curated list of pain points and potential

opportunities to drive positive change

3. Secure collective commitment and prioritization on what to do next

This workshop can ignite the entire composable roadmap initiative. This workshop allows you to guide the group in getting a bunch of great ideas for your team to start implementing.

The participants

Typically, this workshop is delivered between 5-10 stakeholders (too few and you don't get a wide enough picture; too many and people don't get enough mind share). This is a perfect time to engage executives and decision-makers.

The format & outcomes

Ideally, this is a half-day, in-person workshop with a whiteboard and post-its to make it a collaborative session. It can also be done remotely with online collaboration tools over a few weeks. A guided Art of the Possible workshop does the following:

- Identifies the big ideas and key scenarios of your customers' journey
- Discusses your needs, desired outcomes, and how to get

there

- Explores barriers to transitioning
- Identifies implications for integrating transformative technologies into your business
- Connects the dots to current initiatives, investments, and skillsets

Workshop 2: Composable maturity modeling

The Composable Maturity Model workshop guides teams from a basic digital presence to becoming industry leaders in customer experience. It provides a structured framework for assessing composable capabilities, offering a simplified view to improve and personalize the customer journey across multiple omnichannel touchpoints.

The workshop considers composable architecture, omnichannel data, and AI, and introduces the stages that provide a better understanding of an organization's composable capabilities, helping to align marketing strategies with business outcomes more effectively.

- **Enhanced Competitive Edge:** Adopt strategies that set you apart from competitors.

- **How Your MarTech Stacks Up**: Compare your brand across several dimensions to other respondents.
- **Establish a Path Forward:** Learn how brands have sequentially moved up the levels of digital maturity.
- **Industry Leadership:** Compare industry benchmarks in digital experience metrics

This workshop level sets the As-Is, To-be environment across different facets of being composable.

The participants

Typically, this workshop is delivered to 4 to 8 key participants. Key stakeholders often include the executive sponsor, marketing leadership, digital strategy team, developers, and SMEs in relevant business domains.

The format & outcomes

This can be done as a virtual workshop and entails a kickoff meeting, a detailed online survey, and then an executive readout call. This is typically completed within a few weeks. A guided workshop and assessment do the following:

- Provides an industry benchmark

- Identifies gaps and potential risks
- Defines next logical actions

Workshop 3: Product & technology selection

Evaluating, selecting, and implementing modern technologies is becoming more and more difficult. The underlying technologies are quickly changing. Some systems look good on the surface but may not be the best fit. Others may not provide flexibility for the future. Vendor viability, software reliability, and ease of implementation must also be included in the software selection criteria, as well as for other types of composable applications.

Additionally, many software vendors have consolidated or acquired other businesses, and sometimes, it is unclear if a specific platform is really important for the vendor. This can be a problem when considering solutions from vendors that have made large purchases, such as Salesforce, Adobe, Oracle, SAP, Infor, Microsoft, and others. Cloud-based systems also have more layers of complexity. Does the vendor's cloud offering truly provide software as a service (SaaS)? Or is it just an old-fashioned on-premises platform now available in a hosted data center as a managed service? And is that relevant?

The participants

Typically, this is a series of workshops delivered to 4 to 8 key participants. Key stakeholders often include the executive sponsor, marketing leadership, digital strategy team, and IT leadership.

The format & outcomes

These workshops are delivered over 7-9 weeks and are designed to ensure you make informed platform investments with long-term scalability, flexibility, and adoption in mind. Key outcomes include:

- Technology/Platform Evaluation
- Requirement-to-Platform Feature Traceability
- Total Cost of Ownership Comparison
- Technology Recommendation
- Future State Solution Architecture

Workshop 4: Applying generative AI to MarTech investments

Generative AI, and specifically the uses of technologies like ChatGPT and OpenAI, are the fastest-growing conversations among business leaders today. Generative AI continues to be a focus in the Digital Experience community. Many platforms are transforming how digital content is created, managed, and experienced. AI-enhanced tools help Digital Experience leaders to streamline operations, unleash creativity, and drive innovation.

Marketing teams are racing to learn more about generative AI models. There are several conversational LLM transformers that can be used today to create marketing copy, imagery, and personalized advertising.

Workshop objectives:

- Separate the AI hype from value-driving applications
- Better understand how to integrate Gen AI into day-to-day marketing operations
- Quickly leverage Gen AI as a competitive advantage
- Prioritize AI use cases based on risk mitigation

The participants

Typically, this is a series of workshops delivered to 4 to 6 key participants. Key stakeholders often include the executive sponsor, marketing leadership, digital strategy team, and IT leadership.

The format & outcomes

This AI workshop can be done as a virtual workshop and entails a 3-hour meeting and then an executive readout call to discuss recommendations. The guided workshop and feedback analysis deliver the following:

- Prioritized list of use Gen AI cases
- High-Level Action Plan that can enhance existing roadmap

Roadmap checklist: Getting started

People

- ☐ Identify your 'Dream Team'
- ☐ Draft core tenants with IT team/Ops and discuss alignment areas
- ☐ Seek to establish a customer advisory board
- ☐ Develop a pool of 'MACH' partners to interview

Process

- ☐ Determine workshops that align with current gaps
- ☐ Establish timelines / roadmap review cadences / checkpoints
- ☐ Ensure defined KPIs align with near term and short term business goals

Technology

☐ Analyze a short list of 'MACH-centric' technologies

Risk mitigation

☐ Perform TCO analyses on potential investments

☐ Document Tenets with IT/Ops Team

More strategy insights for the journey

From Jonathan Corley, Director of Experience Strategy, Customer Transformation at Sitecore

Adopting a composable martech strategy involves assembling specialized connected software components —each with tailored user interface elements, API services, focused features, etc. — to deliver engaging experiences by aligning digital processes to your organization's unique needs. This focus, shifts away from all-in-one vendor solutions that can lead to underused technology and complex operational challenges.

Adopting composable martech enables your brand to mix-and-match products to suit what your business needs right now. As you're evaluating composable products and capabilities, look for modern cloud-native solutions that provide open and flexible integrations with other software in your stack. Sitecore Connect, for example, has over a thousand integrations to external applications through its visual, no-code integration canvas.

Remember to factor in all related hosting and infrastructure costs that you're dealing with today. Cloud-native solutions fundamentally change cost dynamics of hosting and often dramatically reduce overall run cost.

Digital marketing leaders should prioritize martech solutions that offer a fast path to value, and then assess how these products can meet the specific and unique needs of your business effectively.

If you're operating on an older platform version of a CMS today, you might be evaluating your organization's readiness to invest in a version upgrade versus migrating to a new cloud-native, versionless SaaS CMS.

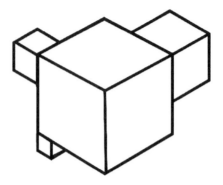

Conclusion

Thanks for joining us on this journey through preparing a composable roadmap. Before beginning on a composable journey of your own, it is important to utilize available resources like this book and other resources to educate yourself and your team on what potential exists for your organization.

Is this the future of marketing?

We believe so. Composable architectures integrated with Gen AI capabilities represent unparalleled flexibility, efficiency and personalization. By adopting a modular approach, businesses can selectively assemble and reconfigure systems to meet evolving demands without overhauling the entire infrastructure. Gen AI enhances this adaptability by automating the creation of content and data analysis, enabling businesses to respond swiftly to market changes and consumer preferences. This synergy not only accelerates innovation but also significantly reduces time-to-market for new services and products.

Moreover, the combination of composable architectures and Gen AI facilitates a more personalized user experience, a critical competitive advantage in today's market. Gen AI can analyze vast amounts of data to deliver highly targeted content and recommendations, improving customer engagement and satisfaction. This personalized approach, supported by the agile nature of composable systems, allows companies to meet specific customer needs while optimizing operational efficiency and resource allocation more effectively. As businesses continue to seek technologies that offer both scalability and customization, composable architectures with Gen AI capabilities will become increasingly indispensable.

Start with your North Star

A North Star Vision is crucial for guiding the strategic implementation of composable architectures in any organization. It serves as a definitive, overarching goal that aligns all efforts and decisions towards a unified objective, ensuring consistency and clarity throughout the process.

It directs the organization's resources and innovation towards areas that offer the most significant impact and value, fostering a culture of continuous improvement and adaptation. This visionary guidance is essential for maintaining focus amid the complexities and evolving nature of technology landscapes, ultimately driving sustained growth and competitive advantage.

Thank you!

We hope this the book equips marketing and IT leaders with the tools and knowledge needed to foster agility, innovation, and connectivity in their operations.

Don't hesitate to contact us if you have questions as you embark on this important step in growing your organization's composable maturity.

We wish you the best on your composable journey.

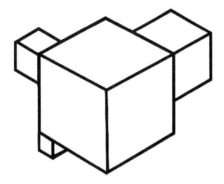

Afterword: Dominik Angerer

Dear Reader,

Congratulations on completing *The Composable Roadmap* by Chad Solomonson and Greg Kihlström! We hope this journey through the intricacies and advantages of composable architecture has been enlightening and inspiring for you. As you've discovered, the concept of composable architecture offers a transformative approach to building digital experiences, providing flexibility, scalability, and agility like never before.

At Storyblok, we understand the challenges and opportunities that marketing professionals face in today's rapidly evolving digital landscape. We've seen firsthand how composable architecture can revolutionize the way organizations create, manage, and deliver content across various channels and touchpoints. As you reflect on the insights shared in this book, we'd like to offer some additional perspectives and guidance tailored specifically for marketing professionals considering a composable approach.

Embracing change and innovation

One of the key takeaways from "The Composable Roadmap" is the importance of embracing change and innovation. In a world where consumer expectations are constantly evolving, organizations must adapt quickly to stay ahead of the curve. Composable architecture emerges as a powerful enabler, allowing marketing teams to engage in seamless experimentation, iteration, and innovation enabling them to respond rapidly to market trends and consumer demands.

As you consider embracing a composable approach within your organization, it's crucial to cultivate a culture of innovation and experimentation, encouraging team members to think creatively and explore fresh ideas. By fostering an innovative culture, you can fully leverage the potential of composable architecture and achieve significant outcomes for your organization. Notably, recent data indicates this shift, with 68% of users migrating to a new CMS in the past three years, and an additional 57% planning to migrate soon. Moreover, studies indicate that switching to a new CMS can yield a potential return on investment (ROI) increase of up to 582%. Stay ahead of the curve by embracing adaptability and innovation in your organizational strategy.

Empowering collaboration across teams

Another critical aspect of composable architecture is its ability to facilitate collaboration across cross-functional teams. By breaking down silos and fostering collaboration between marketing, IT, design, and other departments, organizations can streamline workflows, improve communication, and accelerate time-to-market. As a marketing professional, it's crucial to champion cross-functional collaboration within your organization.

Invest in tools and technologies that foster seamless collaboration and communication across teams. Leverage platforms like Storyblok that enable seamless integration between content management, digital asset management, and other systems to streamline workflows and drive efficiency. But before diving in, consider if your team is equipped with a modern tech stack and if everyone understands how to navigate the new tech landscape. Ensure full team buy-in, from both tech and content/marketing departments, to embrace transformative change. At Storyblok, we prioritize empowering teams, breaking down silos, and facilitating efficient collaboration for success.

Prioritizing flexibility and scalability

Flexibility and scalability are fundamental pillars of composable architecture, essential for organizations to navigate evolving business landscapes and effectively expand their digital presence. As a marketing professional, it's essential to prioritize flexibility and scalability when evaluating technology solutions and designing your digital infrastructure.

Choosing a platform that not only meets current requirements but also boasts the capability to evolve alongside your organization is crucial. Look for solutions that facilitate seamless integration of new features, offer flexibility to integrate with third-party systems, and provide dynamic scalability to accommodate shifting business needs. By placing importance on flexibility and scalability, you lay the foundation for future-proofing your digital infrastructure, ensuring its longevity and adaptability in a rapidly changing environment.

Embracing flexibility enables swift adjustments to meet evolving market demands, while scalability empowers seamless expansion and growth. Together, this fosters agility, allowing your organization to stay ahead of the curve and remain competitive in the digital landscape.

AI-driven marketing

Understanding audience preferences and behavior is essential for delivering engaging content experiences. With Storyblok, our AI features enhance efficiency across content ideation, creation, and management throughout the entire lifecycle. From identifying trends to optimizing content performance, leverage AI to make informed decisions and drive meaningful engagement with your audience. By harnessing the power of AI-driven marketing, marketers can create more personalized and impactful experiences that resonate with their target audience.

Additionally, AI can play a crucial role in data analysis and insights generation. By leveraging AI-powered analytics tools, marketers can gain deeper insights into audience behavior, campaign performance, and content effectiveness, enabling them to make data-driven decisions and optimize their marketing strategies accordingly.

Looking ahead

As you embark on your composable journey, remember that success requires ongoing learning, adaptation, and innovation. Stay curious, stay open-minded, and never stop exploring new possibilities.

In this dynamic landscape, staying ahead requires constant vigilance and a readiness to evolve with the market. Trends shift, consumer behaviors change, and technological advancements reshape the playing field. Those who remain agile and responsive are better equipped to capitalize on emerging opportunities and navigate unforeseen challenges.

The Composable Roadmap by Chad Solomonson and Greg Kihlström, is your trusted guide as you step into the world of composable architecture. It's not just a manual; it offers practical advice and real-world strategies to assist the reader in effectively navigating this approach. Within its pages, you'll discover a roadmap customized to fit your organization's unique needs, without any unnecessary complexity. This guide equips you with the essential information to understand, implement, and embrace composable architecture with confidence. Consider it your go-to resource, providing clear and precise guidance through the twists and turns of this transformative journey.

At Storyblok, we're committed to supporting you every step of the way. Whether you're just starting on your composable journey or seeking to enhance your existing architecture, our dedicated team is here to provide guidance, assistance, and expertise. We understand that each organization is unique, with its own set of challenges and objectives. That's why we offer tailored solutions and personalized support to help you achieve your goals and unlock the full potential of composable architecture.

Together, let's embark on this journey with confidence, knowing that we have the tools, resources, and support needed to succeed.

Warm regards,

Dominik Angerer

CEO & Founder, Storyblok

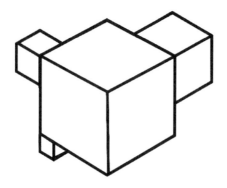

Appendix 1:
Sample composable roadmap

Let's look at a sample composable roadmap, using a retail company as our hypothetical example. The foundation and architecture steps in the roadmap will determine which initiatives should be prioritized.

While we're using a retail example here, you should be able to apply elements of this framework to your own company in any industry.

Example Composable Roadmap for a Retail Company

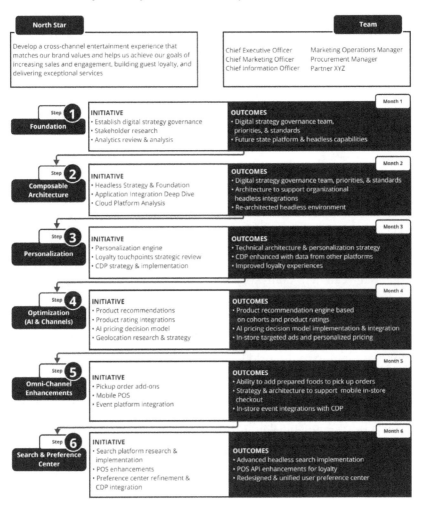

North Star

Develop a cross-channel entertainment experience that matches our brand values and helps us achieve our goals of increasing sales and engagement, building guest loyalty, and delivering exceptional services

Team

Chief Executive Officer
Chief Marketing Officer
Chief Information Officer

Marketing Operations Manager
Procurement Manager
Partner XYZ

Step 1 — Foundation — Month 1

INITIATIVE
- Establish digital strategy governance
- Stakeholder research
- Analytics review & analysis

OUTCOMES
- Digital strategy governance team, priorities, & standards
- Future state platform & headless capabilities

Step 2 — Composable Architecture — Month 2

INITIATIVE
- Headless Strategy & Foundation
- Application Integration Deep Dive
- Cloud Platform Analysis

OUTCOMES
- Digital strategy governance team, priorities, & standards
- Architecture to support organizational headless integrations
- Re-architected headless environment

Step 3 — Personalization — Month 3

INITIATIVE
- Personalization engine
- Loyalty touchpoints strategic review
- CDP strategy & implementation

OUTCOMES
- Technical architecture & personalization strategy
- CDP enhanced with data from other platforms
- Improved loyalty experiences

Step 4 — Optimization (AI & Channels) — Month 4

INITIATIVE
- Product recommendations
- Product rating integrations
- AI pricing decision model
- Geolocation research & strategy

OUTCOMES
- Product recommendation engine based on cohorts and product ratings
- AI pricing decision model implementation & integration
- In-store targeted ads and personalized pricing

Step 5 — Omni-Channel Enhancements — Month 5

INITIATIVE
- Pickup order add-ons
- Mobile POS
- Event platform integration

OUTCOMES
- Ability to add prepared foods to pick up orders
- Strategy & architecture to support mobile in-store checkout
- In-store event integrations with CDP

Step 6 — Search & Preference Center — Month 6

INITIATIVE
- Search platform research & implementation
- POS enhancements
- Preference center refinement & CDP integration

OUTCOMES
- Advanced headless search implementation
- POS API enhancements for loyalty
- Redesigned & unified user preference center

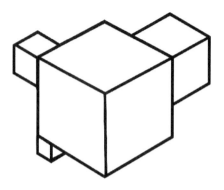

Appendix 2:
Glossary

A glossary can help demystify some of the concepts and terms with composability. This foundational knowledge is important for effectively navigating the transformative ideas presented and applying them to real-world business challenges:

- **Composable:** System or architecture designed to be modular, where components can be selected, assembled, and reconfigured easily. These components are interoperable and can be integrated or replaced without disrupting the overall system, allowing for greater flexibility and agility in adapting to new requirements or technologies.

- **Roadmap:** A strategic plan that outlines a series of steps, milestones, or goals designed to achieve specific objectives over a certain period. It provides a visual guide or a detailed outline of the actions and timelines involved in moving from the current state to a desired future state, helping organizations or individuals navigate and manage progress effectively.

- **Generative AI:** Type of artificial intelligence that can generate new content, such as text, images, or music, by learning from existing data. It uses patterns and features from the data it has been trained on to create new, similar outputs that have not been explicitly programmed.

- **MACH:** An approach to architecture and infrastructure that is Microservices-based, API-first, Cloud-native SaaS, and Headless.

- **Microservices-based:** A microservice is an approach to building an application that breaks down an application's functions into modular, self-contained programs. Microservices make it easier to create and maintain software.

- **API-first:** An application programming interface, or API, is the part of an application that communicates with other applications. APIs are necessary in modern digital infrastructure because they enable standardized and efficient communication between applications, which might differ in function and construction.

- **Cloud-native:** Simply put, this is an application that was designed to reside in the cloud from the start.

- **Headless:** Separates data (the "body") from how it's presented (the "head"), hence the term "headless" and connecting them with APIs.
- **SaaS (Software as a Service):** Allows users to connect to and use cloud-based apps over the Internet.
- **Distributed Cloud:** Offers the ability to store, access, and interact with acquired data using a more dynamic as well as a flexible range of options.
- **Packaged business capabilities:** Software components that represent and perform a well-defined business capability. A PBC combines data schemas, APIs, and event channels into a single entity that can be recognized as such by both technical teams implementing the solution as well as end users of the system.
- **Workshop:** Interactive session focused on discussing, learning, or producing work in a particular area of expertise or on a specific topic. It typically involves a group of participants who engage in intensive discussion and activity on a subject or project under the guidance of a facilitator. Workshops are used to educate, generate ideas, solve problems, or build skills in a collaborative environment.

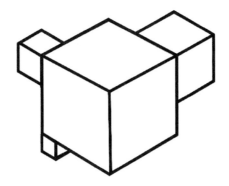

Appendix 3:
Additional resources

In addition to the roadmap and other items provided within this book, there are a few other resources we recommend:

MACH Alliance:

The MACH Alliance is a not-for-profit industry body that advocates for open and best-of-breed enterprise technology ecosystems. They are a vendor-neutral institution that provides resources, education, and guidance through a global community of industry experts to support companies on their journey. The MACH Alliance exists to protect MACH core principles and support buyers on standards, interoperability, and other important considerations when moving from legacy to a composable technology infrastructure. The MACH Certification program is designed to give enterprises confidence that they are choosing best-in-class vendors that can deliver future-proof technology.

You can learn more about the MACH Alliance, certification, membership, and its members at https://www.machalliance.org

The Alliance also offers a MACH Maturity Assessment. It takes less than 10 minutes to complete. At the end, you receive a score and advice on the next steps, with the option to have your results emailed to you to help you get started on your MACH journey. https://machalliance.org/mach-maturity-assessment

The Composable Roadmap website

We have put together some companion materials and will continue to add to them over time at this book's companion website. You can reach that at https://www.thecomposableroadmap.com

RDA

RDA is an award-winning digital consultancy on a mission to build solutions that make a difference. Supported by leading technology partnerships, our digital strategists, industry experts, architects and engineers enable businesses to dream boldly and innovate fearlessly

to deliver value. You can learn more about RDA at
www.rdacorp.com

The Agile Brand

The Agile Brand provides books, podcasts, and other resources for marketing professionals to get the latest insights and best practices. These resources include podcasts, such as the top-ranked enterprise marketing podcast in the world—The Agile Brand with Greg Kihlström—as well as the best-selling Agile Brand Guidebook series, the industry-standard marketing technology wiki, Martechipedia, and more.

You can learn more about The Agile Brand Guide at
https://www.agilebrandguide.com

About the Authors

Chad Solomonson

Chad has over 30 years of entrepreneurial experience at the intersection of marketing and technology. He is passionate about engineering simplicity in our complex and evolving digital marketplace. He has a proven track record of developing go-to-market strategies and programs that build brand awareness, open new markets, launch new products, and strengthen existing client relationships.

Currently, he is the Chief Customer Officer at RDA. He is responsible for developing the firm's strategy, client engagements, and strategic partners. He is focused on the digital consultancy's mission to build solutions that really make a difference through clear, actionable roadmaps so clients know how to act, where to grow, and how to best compete and lead.

Before joining RDA, Chad founded two successful technology startups and held executive marketing, sales, and channel roles at Microsoft, Oracle (Opower), Duke Energy, and Lime Energy.

He often speaks and shares insights on delivering agile roadmaps and emerging AI use cases. He is a 2024 Storyblok Ambassador, Sitecore Ambassador MVP, ADDY Award winner, and Microsoft Partner of the Year winner. He is also a contributing author to one of the best-selling Microsoft books on Portal Collaboration.

Chad also advises brands that are focused on making a positive impact on social or environmental issues, balancing profit with purpose.

Greg Kihlström

Greg Kihlström is a best-selling author, speaker, and entrepreneur and serves as an advisor and consultant to top companies on marketing technology, marketing operations, customer experience, and digital transformation initiatives. He has worked with some of the world's top brands, including Adidas, Coca-Cola, FedEx, HP, Marriott, Nationwide, Victoria's Secret, and Toyota.

He is a multiple-time co-founder and C-level leader, leading his digital experience agency to be acquired by the largest independent marketing agency in the DC region in 2017, successfully exited an HR technology platform provider he co-founded in 2020, and led a SaaS startup to be acquired by a leading edge computing company in 2021. He currently advises and sits on the board of a marketing technology startup.

In addition to his experience as an entrepreneur and leader, he earned his MBA, is currently a doctoral candidate for a DBA in Business Intelligence, and teaches several courses and workshops as a member of the School of Marketing Faculty at the Association of National Advertisers. He has served on the Virginia Tech Pamplin College of Business Marketing Mentorship Advisory Board, the University of Richmond's CX Advisory Board, and was the founding Chair of the American Advertising Federation's National Innovation Committee. Greg is Lean Six Sigma Black Belt certified, an Agile Certified Coach (ICP-ACC), and holds a certification in Business Agility (ICP-BAF).

Greg has written multiple best-selling books, including his 10-part Agile Brand Guides series on marketing technology platforms and practices. His most recent book, the best-selling *House of the Customer* (2023), discusses the 1:1 personalized customer experience of the future and how brands can organize the people, processes, and platforms that enable it. His award-winning podcast, The Agile Brand with Greg Kihlström, now in its 6th year with nearly 500 episodes and millions of downloads, discusses brand strategy, marketing, and customer experience with some of the world's leading experts and leaders.

Greg is a contributing writer to Fast Company, Forbes, MarTech, CustomerThink, and CMSWire and has been featured in publications such as Advertising Age and The Washington Post. Greg has been named #1 on its list of the Top Global Marketing Thought Leaders by Thinkers 360, was named one of ICMI's Top 25 CX Thought Leaders two years in a row, and a DC Inno 50 on Fire as a DC trendsetter in Marketing.

www.ingramcontent.com/pod-product-compliance
Lightning Source LLC
LaVergne TN
LVHW022125060326
832903LV00063B/4113